FAMINE
IN AFRICA

© Aladdin Books Ltd

Designed and produced by
Aladdin Books Ltd
70 Old Compton Street
London W1

First published in
the United States in 1986 by
Gloucester Press
387 Park Avenue South
New York NY 10016

ISBN 0 531 17017 9

Library of Congress Catalog
Card Number: 85-81982

Printed in Belgium

The front cover photograph shows a famine refugee from the Sahel. The back cover photograph shows a young famine victim in Ethiopia.

Contents

ES..ISSUES..ISSU

FAMINE
IN AFRICA

LLOYD TIMBERLAKE

Illustrated by
Ron Hayward Associates

Gloucester Press
New York : Toronto : 1986

Introduction

Famines are getting bigger and lasting longer. Most people think that famine is a direct result of drought. This is only partly true. Many countries like Australia and the US also suffer severe droughts. Some countries, like China and India, once prone to terrible famines, have cured many of their problems. So if people do not starve simply as a result of natural disasters, why are whole countries, particularly in Africa, still dying from famine and disease?

There are many reasons. But basically famine settles on countries where the balance between a population and its ability to feed itself is precarious anyway. Drought, or floods, can easily tip the balance toward famine. But India, with more people and less land than Africa, still manages to feed itself. How?

The explanation is that while nature *triggers* famine, it does not create it. People do that. Countries at peace with themselves are capable of organizing to fight drought. Divided ones cannot. Long-term soil care pays off when drought comes. Abusing and ignoring the soil does not. Growing food crops ensures reserves against a bad harvest. Growing cash crops for industry does not.

And when famine strikes it is not unheard of for a government to deny that it exists in the country and refuse outside help! Usually this happens because it does not wish to create political unrest at home, or upset its financial standing abroad. So famine is a very odd and difficult issue. Right now, millions of Africans are finding out just how difficult.

▽ Many millions of Africans have had to leave their homes and walk hundreds of miles in search of food. These Ethiopians are arriving at a famine relief camp in Sudan.

When is it famine?

In 1985, hunger threatened the lives of 30 million people in Africa. Ten million had abandoned their farms to seek food and water. It was the biggest famine of the century. But even in a "normal" year, 100 million of Africa's 530 million people do not get enough to eat to stay healthy. So when do we say there is a famine?

A famine is when people in a given area who can usually feed themselves suddenly cannot. More people die than usual, especially old people and children. At least 20,000 more children than usual were dying every month in 1985 in western Sudan. But few African countries count their people accurately, so we do not know how many have died overall. The world is often slow to notice famine. It ignored hunger in Ethiopia for three years before a British television crew filmed a famine camp. But that camp in Korem had been there for a long time.

▽ For several years now, huge famine camps like this one at Makalle in Ethiopia, have had to provide emergency shelter for many thousands of starving people.

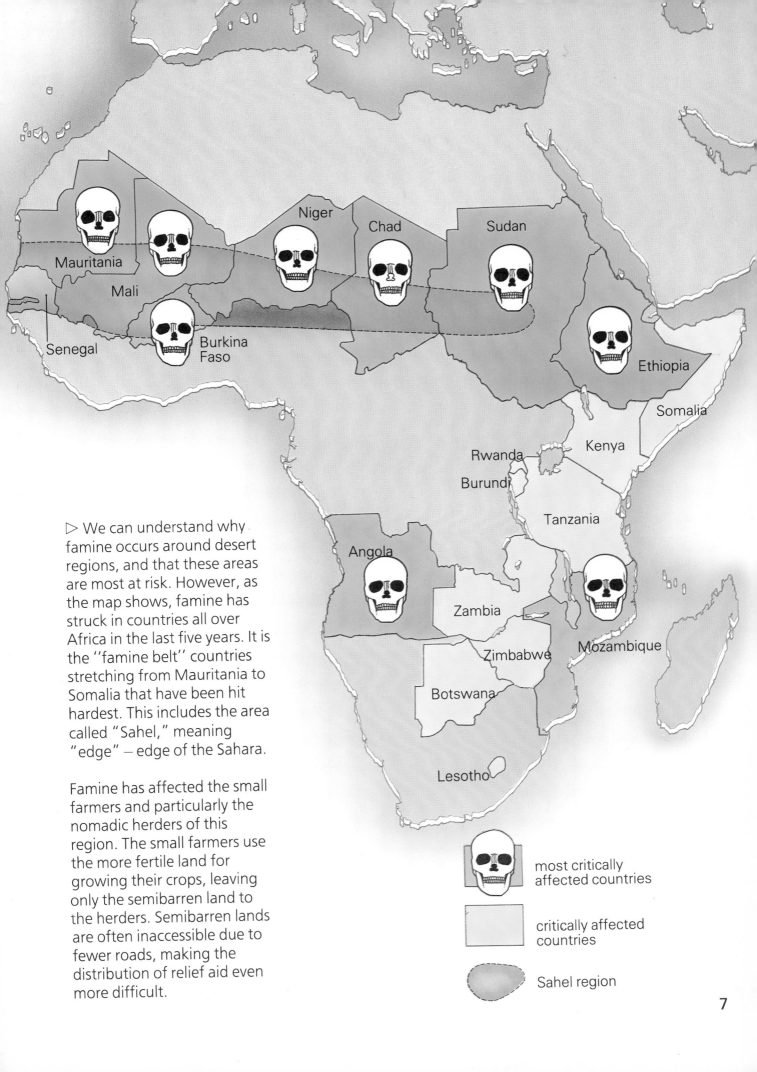

▷ We can understand why famine occurs around desert regions, and that these areas are most at risk. However, as the map shows, famine has struck in countries all over Africa in the last five years. It is the "famine belt" countries stretching from Mauritania to Somalia that have been hit hardest. This includes the area called "Sahel," meaning "edge" — edge of the Sahara.

Famine has affected the small farmers and particularly the nomadic herders of this region. The small farmers use the more fertile land for growing their crops, leaving only the semibarren land to the herders. Semibarren lands are often inaccessible due to fewer roads, making the distribution of relief aid even more difficult.

most critically affected countries

critically affected countries

Sahel region

Creeping disaster

The rains first failed in highland Ethiopia in 1981, and parts of Chad have suffered drought since 1975. But Niger, confidently exporting surplus grain in 1984, was suddenly hungry in 1985. Gradually here, suddenly there, the drought was consistent in one thing: wherever it touched, famine followed. As crops failed, food prices soared, and as fodder disappeared animals and people alike began to starve.

Famine did not spread across Africa; it moved and changed like patterns in a kaleidoscope. But suddenly in 1985 the world was witnessing the worst disaster since the Second World War.

It had happened before. The 1968-73 famine in the Sahel killed perhaps 250,000 people, and the newspapers were suddenly filled with pictures of stick-thin children. Experts noted that the region was drought prone, and a United Nations committee gave sound advice on how to reduce the effect of droughts in the future. But the lessons were not learned.

▽ It does not take much for drought to create famine in Africa. The soil is often poor and farming technology primitive. Crop yields are low anyway, and when harvests fail there are no reserves against famine.

Lack of rain obviously contributes to famine. Yet some parts of Africa get a good deal of rain and still have famine. The reason for this is that rain in Africa is seasonal. It comes all at once – or in some places, not at all. Sudden heavy rain can also cause flooding, washing away soil and crops. It is possible, however, that the Sahel is now getting less rainfall than it got in the past.

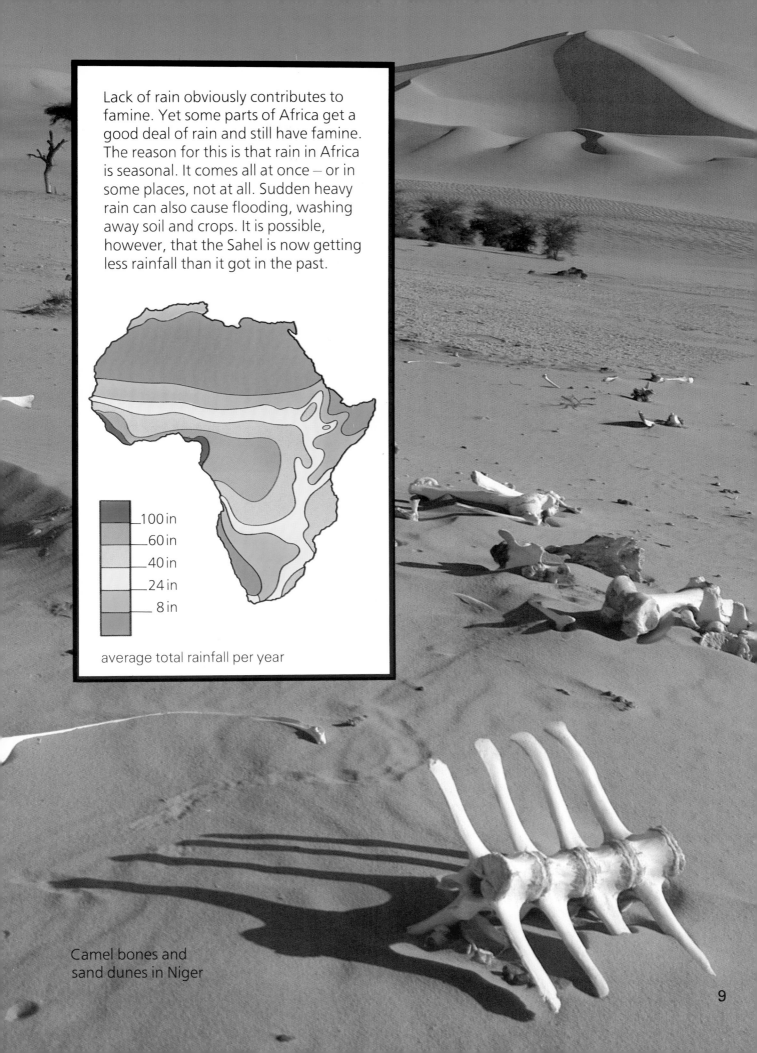

100 in
60 in
40 in
24 in
8 in

average total rainfall per year

Camel bones and
sand dunes in Niger

Flight from the land

Even during a famine, some food is still available – provided you can afford to buy it. If you visited a famine area, *you* wouldn't starve because you would always be able to buy food or exchange something for enough to eat. The people who are starving cannot afford to buy food, and have already sold everything to pay for food.

Most families struggling against hunger follow a similar pattern: when the crops fail, men seek work in town to send money home. Families sell jewelry, then tools, then animals; they buy food and seeds. Only when they have no money and no seed to plant, do they leave home.

But food becomes scarce wherever hungry families go and so even more people become affected by hunger. Famine grows outward like ripples from a stone thrown into a pond. It moves as fast as children and old people can walk. By 1983, hunger had moved from the countryside into the towns along Ethiopia's main road.

▽ Vast numbers of people in the last few years have trekked across Africa in search of food. Listed below are just some of the hunger marches that have happened in one corner of the African famine belt.

1 *1982:* Hungry Ethiopian farmers descend on towns.
2 *1983:* Perhaps 50,000 Ethiopians cross to Somalia and Djibouti.
3 *1983:* 50,000 flee to Sudan.
4 *1984:* 600,000 people cross from Chad into Sudan.
5 *Late 1984:* Famine in Darfur and Kordofan drives Sudanese farmers toward Khartoum and the Nile.
6 *Late 1984:* 700,000 mixed refugees enter Ethiopia because of famine in Somalia. More refugees come from Sudan. Both groups contain Ethiopians escaping from famine in other countries.
7 General drift from war torn Uganda to Sudan.

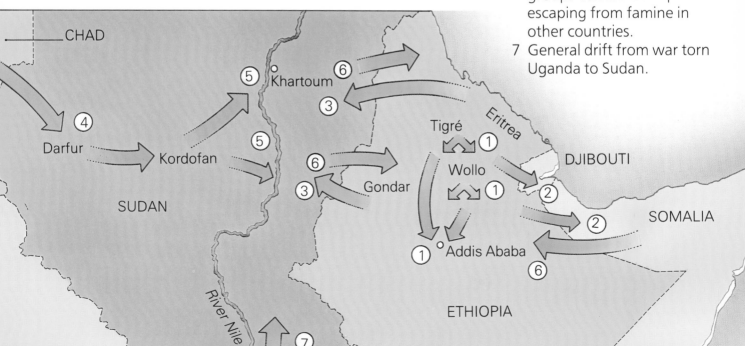

◁ Tigréan refugees crossing into Sudan

In the camps

Thousands of people, far from help of any kind, died quietly. Only a fraction of the starving peasantry made it to the camps. Even so, neither the relief camps nor the capital cities – the other obvious target – were ready for the floods of people that reached them. Wad Sherife camp in eastern Sudan grew from 5,000 to 35,000 in a few months. At nearby Wad Kawli camp, 40,000 had to dig for water in a dry riverbed. In 1984 there was much too little food and medicine in these and other similar camps. Even so, people in the camps were the lucky ones. Things slowly improved, and mortality figures began to fall.

▽ Nouakchott, capital of Mauritania, surrounded by the new shantytown suburbs of drought victims. In the famine of 1968-73, one fifth of the entire Mauritanian population fled the land. Many never went back.

12

The hungry had arrived with little, and had left nothing back home. Many were exhausted from the effects of famine, making them especially vulnerable to disease. And so when rain did fall, it brought cold and new diseases, not relief.

The famine refugees did not wish to stay in the camps; the moment things improved they were prepared to return home. But without seed and oxen, their return would have been futile. Although their governments were anxious to see them return, they did not give them sufficient means. So the camps became a trap; the situation was stalemate.

▽ These children are in Korem Camp, Ethiopia. Even in the camps children and old people have died from normally non-fatal diseases. Their bodies were just too weak to resist them. Diarrhea, measles and malaria have all claimed hundreds of thousands of lives. It is diseases like these that actually cause death rather than starvation itself.

Manmade deserts

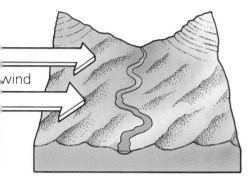

△ Overcultivation: Farmers plant on soil too poor, on hills too steep, in areas too dry. They try to get more from the soil than it can give.

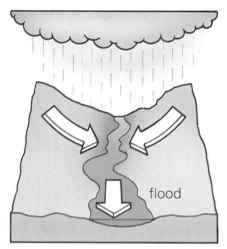

wind

△ Wind erosion: Wind takes away topsoil, leaving sand or rock. Wind also pushes dunes ahead of it.

flood

△ Flash-flooding: Overused soil has few plants to help bind the soil and slow rainfall. So it is swept away.

Most African soils are poor at the best of times. The land needs fertilizer, or a rest between crops to regain nutrients. But few farmers can afford fertilizer, and rapid population growth means that big, hungry families cannot let land rest between crops. They must plant even poorer, drier soils that should never be planted in the first place. So the soil is overused. Exposed to wind and water, topsoil is eroded away by both. Farmland begins to look like desert. So across the Sahel, the Sahara seems to be moving south. But as a farmer said: "We are *pulling* it south."

Sowing millet in a "field," Mauritania

14

It is hard to change this cycle without spending money — money farmers don't have. In Burkina Faso, a farmer may earn 16 dollars a month. He cannot afford fertilizer, much less a diesel pump to irrigate his land.

But there are solutions. In Niger, farmers have planted long lines of trees to stop wind erosion; they now grow much more food. Niger has laws against farmers planting crops too far north, since these would exhaust the fragile soil and lay the soil open to desert. Unfortunately, in remote areas these laws cannot always be enforced.

▽ Sand dunes move ahead of the wind. But they can be stopped by building fences of stalks and planting drought-resistant grasses and trees. In China vast schemes like this have tripled crop yields in some coastal regions which were turning to desert.

Lost forests

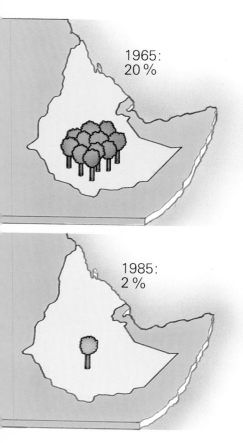

Trees have a far greater significance in the famine story than we might imagine. Planting windbreaks is a minor thing, compared with the fact that if there were sufficient trees, the effect of droughts could be greatly reduced. The roots of trees bind the soil together and when rain water is gently introduced into the soil by the leaves, it is kept there by the roots. Sufficient trees keep terraces in place and help the soil resist flash-flooding. Unfortunately, across Africa people are cutting down forests to create new farmland and for fuel, far faster than they are replacing them.

△ Twenty years ago, 20 percent of Ethiopia was under forest. Now it is only 2 percent. Across Africa the forests are being leveled at the rate of 6.7 million acres (2.7 million hectares) every year.

▷ Terraced farmlands like these in the Ethiopian highlands are doubly exposed. The soil is thin and lacking in cover and support from trees.

16

Farmers know they must plant trees, but tree-planting time is also grain-planting time. Young trees must be guarded from hungry animals. Who has time to do this? And you cannot just plant trees on steep hills, you must dig terraces, so that the young trees won't be washed away. The UN pays Ethiopian farmers in food to "reforest." They have planted five million trees and built enough terraces to stretch almost to the Moon and back. But it is only a small beginning — the whole scheme needs to be fifty times greater and across the whole of North Africa as well.

▽ A tree called Acacia albida is often planted in reforestation schemes. In periods of drought its long roots can tap water deep underground. Also, this tree, unlike those around it, has leaves during the dry season. These leaves provide shade and fodder for cattle. And when a sudden hard rain falls, the wide canopy and deep roots protect the soil around the tree.

canopy provides fodder and shade

rain falls gently on soil

roots bind the soil and tap water

Hungry herds

There are between 15 and 24 million people living off herds of grazing animals in the dry parts of Africa. The land is too poor to support regular harvests, but since the herds are mobile they can graze wherever rain may fall. And in recent years, various aid programs have improved the herders' lot by digging deep wells across the Sahel and eastern Africa.

Unfortunately, when drought struck, two things happened. No amount of wells could provide fodder, and it was of hunger rather than thirst that the herds began to die. Secondly, the herders stayed close to the new wells and the surrounding areas became badly overgrazed, even by normal standards.

Large herds grazing on the edge of the desert have been blamed for damaging the land, helping the process of "desertification." But where else are they to go? In the Sahel and many other parts of Africa, all the good land has been taken by crop farmers.

▽ It was to wells like these that the nomadic herders clung during the drought. Overcrowding sometimes led to armed clashes between rival groups.

18

The Afar people are herders in the Ethiopian lowlands. Once they had grasslands along the Awash River. But the government dammed the river to provide irrigation for sugar and cotton farms. The grasslands disappeared.

So when a drought struck in 1972-74 nearly a third of the Afar starved to death. But afterward, good grazing land remained scarce, and in the drought in 1980 they began to die again.

Thousands of Afar took their cattle into the drought-stricken highlands. At least there was more growing up there than in the lowlands. But they found the area already crowded and the farmers also going hungry.

The Afar, like most nomads, carry guns. Fighting soon broke out between nomad and farmer. No one knows how many died. Eventually, trapped in a valley, the Afar watched their herds die.

Pathetic attempts to sell the hides of the dead animals came to nothing. There were hides for the taking all across the famine belt.

The Afar was not an isolated case. The Burana people of Burkina Faso lost 70 percent of their cattle; the Turkana of Kenya even more.

Only food aid could save the nomads when drought came. Many did not get it.

Food or cash?

In addition to all of these problems, many experts believe Africa is being farmed in the wrong way. African governments need "foreign exchange" – dollars. To get them they must grow something that will sell abroad. So they grow "cash" crops like coffee, cocoa, sugar and cotton, giving farmers loans and paying good prices for these harvests. Cash crops are grown on the best land, so small farmers may be pushed onto poorer soil to make way for big irrigation schemes and plantations. Harsh, perhaps, but profitable, and in 1984 five countries in the Sahel had record cotton harvests – in the middle of a drought!

▽ Coffee beans spread out to dry in Kenya. The price paid for African coffee has been falling: from $2.00 paid per pound between 1975-80, to $1.40 in 1982, and possibly only $1.20 in 1985.
And the rising strength of the dollar has *not* helped, as the cost of foreign goods needed has risen proportionately.

However, in the same year those five countries had to import record amounts of grain. The farmers had been too busy growing cotton and not enough food. Moreover, the food crops did not pay well. The governments made sure that prices were kept low so that people in the cities – who kept them in power – had cheap food. Unfortunately, imported food was cheaper still. Northern countries were happy to sell their surplus food for very little. So the food farmers got poorer and cash cropping went on. Many countries gambled on a single crop – and when world prices began to fall, they faced disaster.

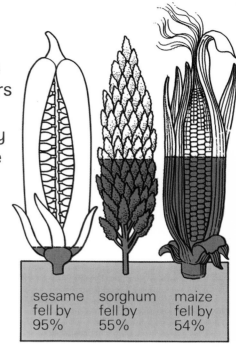

| sesame fell by 95% | sorghum fell by 55% | maize fell by 54% |

△ The diagram illustrates the staggering drop in food production in Kordofan province, Sudan, between 1961-73.

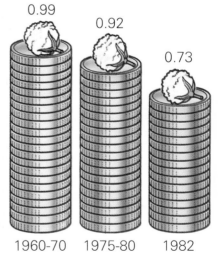

0.99　　0.92　　0.73

1960-70　　1975-80　　1982

△ The figures show dollars paid per pound of cotton over the years. The drop in value is unfortunate for countries such as Chad, which depends on cotton for 80 percent of its foreign exchange.

Growing chaos

Almost 12 billion dollars went in aid to the Sahel during 1974-82. How was it used?

△ 4.2 billion dollars went on food imports, paying officials, and government expenses.

△ 4.2 billion dollars were spent on construction work, education, health and communications.

△ 3.59 billion dollars were invested in industry and other commercial projects.

△ Only 660,000 dollars went to unirrigated food farms and on reforestation.

Much of Africa is actually becoming steadily less "developed." There are many reasons for this, but bad planning is high on the list. When African countries gained independence many chose to develop industry and cities rather than food farming. It was a bad decision. For as food production fell, the population of Africa, especially in the cities, rose faster than anywhere else in the world. To feed the cities, foreign food, wheat and rice had to be imported, changing the tastes of the increasingly westernized city dwellers and creating even more of a gulf between town and country.

▽ The Organization of African Unity building, Addis Ababa, Ethiopia. The idea of African countries working together is a good one, but many people question whether money should be spent on showpiece buildings. Is this the best use for it?

So the farmers, still the majority of the population, stayed poor, too poor to buy the products of the new industries. Nor did the outside world buy much. Late in the day plans were made to improve the land, but without involving the farmers! As a result, schemes developed in the cities, by foreign experts, often went wrong. (In India, where farmers have a real voice in government, schemes have more chance of success.) Add to this frequent changes of government, civil wars and corruption, and it is not difficult to see why foreign banks and governments are reluctant to invest in Africa.

▽ In many African countries more money is spent on weapons than on tackling the food problem. Ethiopia went further, actually staging lavish political celebrations in the middle of the famine.

Mixed blessings

Africa gets two kinds of help from outside; long-term development aid and emergency relief. Even if its development aid were shared equally, every African would get just 20 dollars a year. But the money goes to governments, not people, and we have seen how governments may spend it unwisely. Nor is aid quite what it seems. The aid-giving governments like their money spent on big projects, like roads and dams. Then experts and materials have to be used and paid for. Who supplies these things? The aid-giving countries.

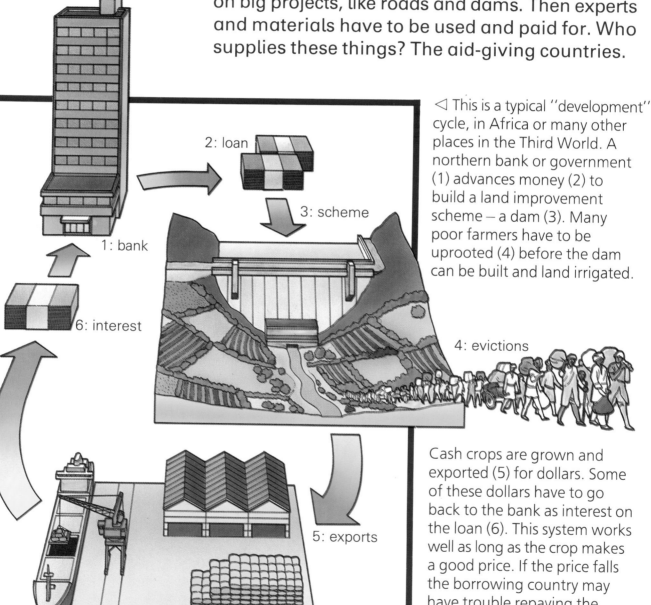

2: loan

3: scheme

1: bank

6: interest

4: evictions

5: exports

◁ This is a typical "development" cycle, in Africa or many other places in the Third World. A northern bank or government (1) advances money (2) to build a land improvement scheme – a dam (3). Many poor farmers have to be uprooted (4) before the dam can be built and land irrigated.

Cash crops are grown and exported (5) for dollars. Some of these dollars have to go back to the bank as interest on the loan (6). This system works well as long as the crop makes a good price. If the price falls the borrowing country may have trouble repaying the interest. So more money may have to be borrowed to grow something else.

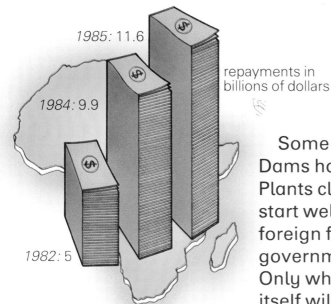

1985: 11.6

1984: 9.9

1982: 5

repayments in
billions of dollars

△ Debts, and interest on
debts, is crippling Africa. Every
year more of its income goes
on repaying foreign debts.

Some of these schemes are not even practical.
Dams hold back rich silt from farms downriver.
Plants clog up reservoirs. And some schemes
start well, but fail through neglect. Finally, cheap
foreign food has discouraged African
governments from tackling the real problem.
Only when Africa can grow enough food to feed
itself will the famines end. Some people want to
stop sending food to Africa – except in famines.
But if development aid was spent wisely,
emergency relief aid might not be needed.

Spraying a dam reservoir to kill water hyacinth in Sudan

Feeding the hungry

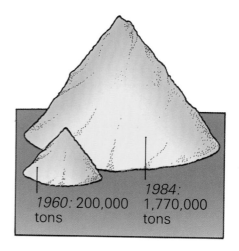

By 1985 a guilty world was shipping mountains of free grain to the famine belt. There were too few African ports to handle this sudden flood. However, getting the food from the docks to people starving hundreds of miles away was an even bigger problem. There are few good roads, and trucks were scarce – or being used for other things, like war. Ethiopia alone needed 120,000 tons of grain every month, but only 50,000 tons were getting through.

Getting food into the landlocked nations was even harder. When a bridge carrying the only railroad into western Sudan collapsed, over a million people faced starvation. Instead of getting the 1,000 tons of grain they needed every day, these people had been getting only 260 tons. Now with the railroad gone, they were down to a daily airlift of 70 tons.

The situation is worsened as governments at war with their own people favor certain regions and conceal from relief agencies where the famine is worst.

1960: 200,000 tons   *1984:* 1,770,000 tons

△ The Sahel imported only 200,000 tons of grain in 1960. In 1984 it needed 1,700,000 tons – and 19 million people depended on it.

▷ Hungry refugees from Tigré patiently wait to be fed in a camp at Tokalabab.

▽ The present crisis has drawn many air forces together to airlift food. But even the huge Hercules transporters can only carry 21 tons at a time.

Can things change?

The African famine is bleak, but its bleakness may bring changes. Governments across Africa are realizing they cannot stay in power with their people dying by the thousands. They are looking to the farmers and their needs. Zimbabwe was a "drought country" in early 1985. A few months later it was donating corn to Ethiopia. The farmers were getting good prices for their grain, government loans, fertilizer at a cheap price and help in selling their harvests. Across the drought belt, farmers were forming groups to plant trees, dig simple irrigation systems and build terraces. Scientists were working on drought-resistant sorghum and millet varieties.

The big struggle will be to turn all the charity going to Africa into the sort of aid that will make future charity unnecessary. But will the governments, African and Northern, see reason?

△ Sorghum in Ethiopia takes nine months to ripen. There is now a new type of sorghum that ripens in 12 weeks.

▽ Digging irrigation ditches in Tigré. Through simple things like this countries like India are now food self-sufficient.

New life for the desert in Chad

Hard facts

Famine worldwide

Nigeria 1967-1970

After two and a half years of war in the eastern region, Biafra, 2 million people were estimated dead, the majority from starvation and disease. Starvation was so acute that many people were reduced to eating vermin, bought at high prices in the markets.

Kampuchea 1970

According to some reports, 10 million people lost their homes as the Khmer Rouge struggled for power in the years 1970-75. 500,000 Cambodians died and no one knows how many have perished since from starvation and disease – estimates are as high as 3 million.

Ethiopia 1972-74

As many as 200,000 from a population of 27 million died in the famine. The famine happened at a time when there was no unusual reduction in food output. However, many people were too poor to buy food from other parts of Ethiopia.

Bangladesh 1974

Following severe floods, the price of rice rose sharply. At one stage nearly six thousand camps were providing free food relief to 4.35 million people, 6 percent of the population. Thousands of people died of starvation – perhaps as many as 100,000.

Peru 1983

Floods devastated many roads and homes in the northern region of Peru. Bridges, health posts and schools suffered severe damage. Irrigation channels were also destroyed by the flood water, threatening agriculture for years to come.

Bolivia 1983

An acute shortage of potato and other seed affected 1.6 million people, a quarter of the country's population. Severe drought and the low reserves from previous harvests forced people to react to the disaster by crowding into the cities.

---

200 years of famine

1783 A volcano erupts and causes Iceland's worst famine. Crops are destroyed as the land is covered with ash. 10,000 people die – one fifth of Iceland's population.

1845-51 Famine sweeps Ireland as the potato crop fails due to disease. The famine kills about one fifth of the Irish population and leads to the emigration of many others.

1888-92 The "Great Ethiopia Famine" kills as many as a third of the population. Loss of cattle due to disease means the peasants are unable to plow and prepare their land. Added to this, the failure of the rains creates starvation on a horrific scale.

1930 Mass starvation in Russia kills 3 million people, mainly in the Ukraine. Many peasants, resisting changes in government farm policy, actually burn their own grain supplies.

1943 The last major famine in India, the "Great Bengal Famine," causes about 3 million deaths. A cyclone, followed by torrential rain and a fungus disease, badly affected the winter crop of rice in 1942. However, rice production and wheat importation in India as a whole is not greatly reduced.

1946-48 China suffers its worst famine, affecting 30 million people.

Africa today

Angola
Some 500,000 of Angola's people need relief, and severe cold in some areas has made conditions especially bad: one out of three children is dying before the age of five. Fighting between two rebel groups and pressure from South Africa has increased the hardship.

Botswana
At least 80 percent of Botswana's population is in need of urgent relief, after the country has suffered from four years of drought. The area of land under crops is only one tenth of previous years. The government is using much of its budget for relief work.

Burkina Faso
Some 500,000 of the population affected. In many areas the failure of the crops has been total. The nation urgently needs vaccines to protect against disease. Fertilizers, tools and work animals are also needed to improve agriculture.

Cape Verde
This is a tiny island nation that has suffered drought since 1975. The severe water shortages have meant that only 20 percent of the population get enough water. The situation is so serious that there has been some talk of abandoning the islands.

Chad
Chad has been suffering its "worst drought ever." About 1,000 people have been dying every month in 1985 and 1.5 million need urgent relief. Yet in 1984, the grain harvest covered half the nation's needs. Many refugees have fled from Chad to Sudan.

Kenya
Over 11 percent of Kenya's population is affected by famine and needs food relief. The usually productive highlands and the eastern regions have also suffered crop failures. Kenya is wealthier and better organized than some African nations.

Mali
This is one of the hardest nations to reach with emergency food aid. Drought has now affected the country for many years and in 1985 1.2 million of the population were hungry, with cereal production halved and many herds dead.

Mozambique
2.5 million people are affected and infant deaths are among the world's highest. Civil war has made relief work and the replanting of the land difficult; war has also destroyed schools and clinics. The government of Mozambique was slow to react to the famine.

Niger
Niger is suffering its worst drought of the century, affecting 2.5 million people in 3,270 villages. 400,000 people are homeless. Water supplies are a special problem; relief workers are digging new wells and deepening old ones in an attempt to create new supplies.

Somalia
Remaining crops have suffered badly from an invasion of worms. The two main rivers, the lifelines of the nation, are too low to allow for irrigation of the land. Some civil strife in the north has caused further problems. Yet rains in 1985 gave the nation new hope.

Sudan
Regular rains failed to fall in late 1984. Since then tens of thousands of rural people have poured into the towns and suburbs along the banks of the Nile as their crops failed. The Sudanese government was extremely slow to admit to the famine to the outside world.

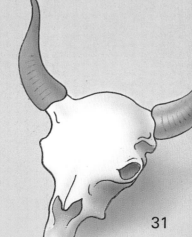

31

Index

Photographic Credits:
Cover and page 15, FAO; pages 4/5, 10, 16/17,
23, 28 and back cover, Mike Goldwater/
Network; page 6, Magnum/F. Scianna; page 8,
Oxfam; pages 9 and 20/21, Bruce Colman;
pages 12, 13, 14, 26 and 27, John Hillelson;
pages 18 and 19, Susan Griggs; pages 22, 25
and 29, Robert Harding; back cover,
John Hillelson Agency.

Acknowledgements
The publishers would like to gratefully
acknowledge the valuable assistance given by
Friends of the Earth and Earthscan in the
preparation of this series. And thanks to the
United Nations Information Centre, the United
Nations High Commissioner for Refugees and
Mark Mallock-Brown of the Economist.

PRINTED IN BELGIUM BY
proost
INTERNATIONAL BOOK PRODUCTION